# JANE DÁVILA'S
# Surface Design
## Essentials

- Explore Paints, Mediums, Inks & Pencils
- 15 Techniques for Fabrics & More

## JANE DÁVILA

C&T PUBLISHING

Text and artwork copyright © 2010 by Jane Dávila

Artwork copyright © 2010 by C&T Publishing, Inc.

Publisher: Amy Marson

Creative Director: Gailen Runge

Acquisitions Editor: Susanne Woods

Editor: Lynn Koolish

Technical Editor: Teresa Stroin

Copyeditor/Proofreader: Wordfirm Inc.

Cover/Book Designer: Kristen Yenche

Production Coordinator: Casey Dukes and Kirstie L. Pettersen

Production Editor: Julia Cianci

Quilt photography by Christina Carty-Francis and Diane Pedersen of C&T Publishing, Inc., unless otherwise noted.

How-to photography by Jane Dávila unless otherwise noted.

Published by C&T Publishing, Inc., P.O. Box 1456, Lafayette, CA 94549

Library of Congress Cataloging-in-Publication Data

Dávila, Jane.

Jane Dávila's surface design essentials : explore paints, mediums, inks & pencils : 15 techniques for fabrics & more / Jane Dávila.

p. cm.

ISBN 978-1-60705-077-3

1. Textile painting. 2. Quilts. 3. Art quilts. I. Title. II. Title: Surface design essentials.

TT851.D386 2010

746.6--dc22

Printed in China

10 9 8 7 6 5 4 3 2

*el melon,* **made by Jane Dávila, 5″ × 5″**

**Quilt made with found paper, acrylic paint wash, and art paper adhered with gel medium**

# DEDICATION

For my parents, Richard and Claire Oehler, for instilling in me an endless curiosity about the world around me and for believing that I can do anything.

I would like to thank everyone at C&T, including Diane Pedersen for her patience and expertise and most especially my partners in paint on this project, Mary Wruck and Lynn Koolish.

# CONTENTS

# INTRODUCTION
# TO SURFACE DESIGN

Surface design is by definition the application of designs and processes to fabric, paper, or other surfaces. Knowing how to customize surfaces in a variety of ways allows you to create unique art that is infused with your personal vision and creative spirit.

The techniques, ideas, and materials shown in this book will expand your horizons, whether you are a quilter, a fiber artist, or a mixed-media artist, and whether you are an experienced pro or just getting started on the surface design adventure. I've included basics, techniques, projects, and a gallery to inspire you and get you started. Happy accidents occur while playing with new techniques—so don't be afraid to try things out or create variations on these ideas and see where they lead you!

The materials used for the techniques and projects in this book (soft-body acrylic paint, acrylic ink, acrylic mediums, and water-soluble ink pencils) all clean up with regular soap and water and are much, much safer to use than solvent-based products or those that must be used with chemicals. The techniques presented here are all low-tech and require only everyday, easy-to-find supplies. I try very hard to limit my exposure to toxic processes, fumes, and materials, so acrylic paints, inks, and mediums are ideal. Additionally, their impact on the environment is negligible compared to paints made with petroleum-based solvents, processes that release toxic fumes into the air, and cleanup that requires harmful chemicals. Acrylics are very easy to use, whether you have experience with them or not, and are perfect for use on fabric and paper. The possibilities are endless!

Let's get started!

*la luna,* made by Jane Dávila, 4˝ × 6˝

**Block print made with acrylic paint and art paper adhered with gel medium**

# SURFACE DESIGN BASICS

## Color Mixing

While paints are available in many colors, knowing how to mix your own colors means that you can create the exact colors you need. Mixing colors successfully requires a little bit of practice and some knowledge of how colors work together.

**NOTE**

*There are advantages to finding and using a color straight out of a bottle:*

- *The color is consistent (every bottle you buy will be the same).*
- *You don't need to keep mixed colors from drying out.*
- *You have larger quantities of the desired color.*

Red, yellow, and blue, the three colors that can't be made by mixing other colors, are known as primary colors.

**Red, yellow, blue**

Mixing two primary colors together results in a secondary color (orange, violet, or green).

**Red + yellow = orange**

**Blue + red = violet**

**Yellow + blue = green**

The proportions in which you add the primaries will result in different secondaries. For example, if you use more yellow and less blue to make a green, you will make a yellowish or lime green.

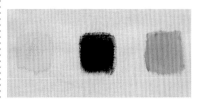
**Lots of yellow + a little bit of blue = lime green**

**✳ TIP**

Experiment by creating secondary colors with varying amounts of primaries, and keep your results in a notebook.

Adding white to a color creates a tint. It lightens the color but also tends to make it cooler and less vibrant.

**Red + white = pink**

Adding black to a color creates a shade. Black should be used very sparingly when mixing colors, as not a lot is needed to darken a color.

*(Red + black = burgundy swatch)*

**Red + black = burgundy**

The easiest way to create neutral browns is to mix together a secondary color and the primary color that wasn't used in making it (also known as its complement). For example, orange is made from red and yellow, so if you add blue to orange you make brown. Each of the secondaries combined with its other primary will create a slightly different brown. Varying the proportions of each will also yield different results. It is worthwhile to take notes and paint swatches in a notebook for future reference.

**Violet + yellow = a cool brown**

**Green + red = a warm brown**

**Orange + blue = an olive brown**

Grays also contain all three primary colors plus the addition of white. The easiest way to make a gray is to mix orange, blue, and white, using more blue than either of the other two. Add more white for a lighter gray; add more blue for a darker gray.

**Orange + blue + white = gray**

**✳ TIP**

- If you mix too many colors together, you get mud. If you don't want mud, start over. It's much easier to begin again than to try to fix a bad color.

- Always add a dark color to a light one. You will always need less of a dark color than a light one when mixing.

# Using a Palette

A palette can be very helpful when mixing colors. There are different types of palettes, and some are better suited to some materials than others. For example, a palette with wells is used with liquid colors, such as inks.

Palettes are available in a variety of sizes and shapes and with a variety of sizes and shapes of wells.

Acrylic paints, because they are thicker, can be mixed on either flat or welled palettes.

Palette and disposable palette paper

Some palettes are perfect for mixing secondaries from primaries.

Use a different brush for each color.

When mixing a range of colors for blending, use a palette with many wells.

Start with the two main colors at either end, and create the mixes in between.

Lay out the colors on the palette in an order that makes sense to you as you're painting—for example, group warm colors and cool colors together, or dark and lighter colors together.

Colors are ready to use.

If you don't use all the colors that you mixed in one sitting, you will need a way to prevent them from drying out. Some palettes have covers that seal the colors to keep air out. If your palette doesn't have a cover, you can create a seal over the paint with plastic wrap.

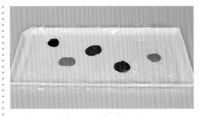

Sealing a palette with plastic wrap

A sealed palette with a cover

You can also mix paint on parchment paper. Place the parchment paper over damp paper towels, and place it all in a sealable, airtight container. The moisture in the paper towel will keep the paint fresh for a week or longer.

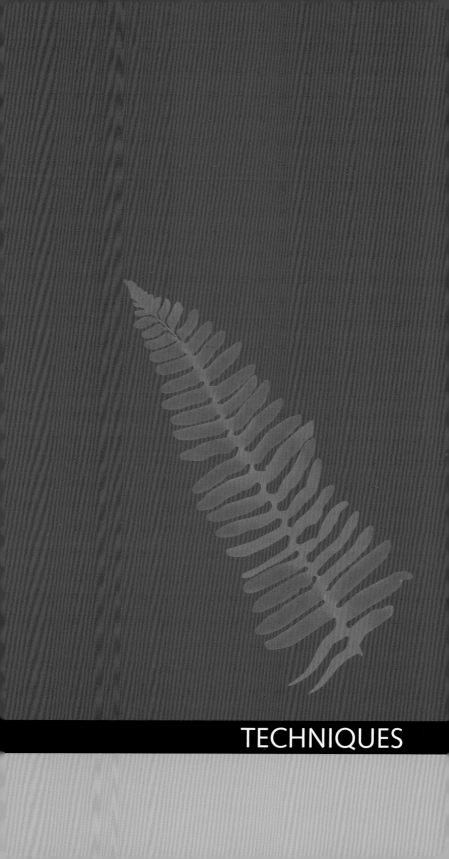

TECHNIQUES

Motif painted with soft-body acrylic paint, accented with water-soluble ink pencils (pages 42–43) and stitching

If you plan to create your design with a paintbrush, there are several ways to get the design onto fabric.

- Paint the design freehand, directly on the fabric.

- Draw a design on paper, and, if the fabric is light enough, place the fabric on top of the drawing and trace using a fine, sharp pencil or a mechanical pencil. Then paint the design.

- If the fabric is too dark to see through, place the drawing on top of the fabric and slip a sheet of artist transfer paper, such as Saral (available at art supply stores), in between. Trace over the drawing on the paper again, and the design will transfer onto the fabric underneath. Then paint the design.

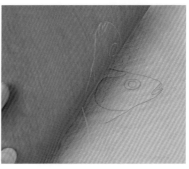

## BLENDING COLORS

Create a blending effect by starting with two colors at opposite ends of a palette (page 7). Between the two ends, create 3–5 mixes of the colors .

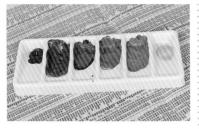

Working quickly, apply the colors to the fabric, blending where the colors meet or overlap.

## ADDING TEXTURE

Texture and interest can be added to paint that has been applied as a background or base.

- Apply a second color with a natural sponge. Rotate the sponge slightly each time you press down to avoid creating a repeating pattern.

- Create a scumbling effect by dragging a dry brush across one color, leaving a thin, uneven layer of another color.

- Splatter colors on top of other colors by using a toothbrush dipped in paint and flicking it over the fabric. Protect your work area—this one can be messy!

One color is painted on and allowed to dry. A second color, very slightly diluted with water, is added along one edge and the piece is placed at an angle to allow the color to drip.

One color is painted on and allowed to dry. A second color is randomly applied with a palette knife.

One color is painted on and allowed to dry. Masking tape cut into small squares is taped in a pattern over the dried paint. A second color is applied. Once this layer of paint is dry, the masking tape is removed to reveal the design.

One color is painted on and allowed to dry. A second color is applied with a rag.

One color is painted on and allowed to dry. A second color is applied with a flat object like a spatula or an old credit card by scraping the color across, revealing most of the under color.

Painted fabric adhered to a background with acrylic medium, accented with water-soluble pencil (pages 42–43)

Acrylic mediums can be added to paint or ink in order to change their behavior. They can also be used to seal, adhere, or coat surfaces, as well as to create textures (alone or with paint) and to capture objects and hold them to surfaces. Two of my favorites are fabric medium and matte gel medium.

## FABRIC MEDIUM

Fabric medium is added to acrylic paint primarily to change the way the paint feels when it dries on the fabric. Acrylic paint tends to be a little stiff when dry, and the fabric medium helps keep the hand of the painted fabric soft. It also helps control bleeding and enhances the flow and workability of the paint or ink. Fabric medium increases the volume of paint without affecting the color and enhances the durability of the painted fabric. Adding it to ink thickens the ink to a consistency closer to acrylic paint, without changing the color.

Mix fabric medium with soft-body acrylic paint in a 1:1 formula. Test your results on fabric. Add more paint for a heavier, more opaque application; add more medium for a thinner, more translucent appearance.

Left: more fabric medium, less paint; right: more paint, less fabric medium

## MATTE GEL MEDIUM

Matte gel medium is extremely versatile and has many uses. Added to soft-body acrylic paint or ink, it increases the "open time," or the length of time it takes paint or ink to dry. This is very useful when you are creating an image with blended colors. When dry, matte gel medium is water-resistant and permanent. Matte gel medium can be used to create image transfers (pages 46–48). It is also a superior adhesive—you can attach paper or other found objects to fabric to create collages. It's easy to sew through when dry. When used as a topcoat, it protects the covered items from water and light, as well as abrasion. Coat very porous surfaces with matte gel medium to seal those surfaces before applying paint or ink. You can also use matte gel medium to create a fusible (described below).

## FABRIC FUSIBLE

1. Coat the back side of the fabric you'd like to adhere with a thin, even coat of matte gel medium, and allow to dry thoroughly.

**2.** Once the matte gel medium is completely dry, cut the coated fabric into any shape with scissors or a rotary cutter. Place the coated shape onto a background (medium side down), and cover with a pressing sheet or piece of parchment paper. Iron to heat the medium, creating a permanent bond.

## 🐦 NOTE

*Some advantages to this method are that you don't need to decide ahead of time which fabrics should have fusible interfacing applied to them (you can add matte gel medium to the fabric at any time), the treated fabrics will keep indefinitely until needed, and any fraying of raw edges will be very minimal.*

## USING MEDIUMS TO CAPTURE OBJECTS

Matte gel medium and fabric medium can be used to capture and hold small objects to fabric and other surfaces. The mediums will dry clear and allow the objects to be completely visible.

- For bulky objects, like small glass beads, apply a thick layer of gel medium to your surface. Pour or place beads into fresh medium

and tap lightly to ensure good adhesion. Thick layers of medium will take a few hours to a full day to dry, depending on a number of factors, including the humidity in the air.

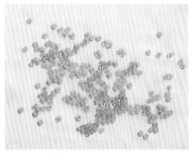

It can be difficult to apply more medium, if needed, on top of objects like beads without the beads sticking to your paintbrush, so make sure you apply enough medium as a base.

- Add snips of threads and yarns to fabric by applying a layer of gel medium with a paintbrush or foam brush. Add thread and yarn to fresh medium. Apply more gel medium over the threads and yarn if necessary. Cover with a piece of parchment paper and press down with your hands to ensure good adhesion. Remove parchment paper to allow to dry.

If you plan to sew over the snipped threads and yarn, keep the layer of gel medium fairly thin.

- Sprinkle glitter into fresh medium to add permanent sparkle to your surfaces.

This can be a particularly nice effect in landscape quilts.

Apply the medium randomly or in an intentional design. You can also apply medium with a stamp.

## USING MEDIUMS TO ADD TEXTURE

Permanent texture can be added to fabric and other surfaces with gel medium and paint or ink.

- Add acrylic paint or ink to matte gel medium. Apply a thick layer of the mixture to your surface. Use a brush to create raised areas in the mixture.

Experiment with the many kinds of subtle or obvious texture.

- Mix equal parts of matte gel medium and clean sand. Add acrylic paint or ink to the sand mixture. Apply a layer of this mixture to your surface and allow to dry.

- Apply matte gel medium through a textural object, like a piece of screen or rubber shelf liner. Allow it to dry completely. Brush acrylic paint over the surface of the dried, textured medium and wipe most of it away from the raised areas with a rag.

If desired, add another color to the raised areas of the design.

- Mix acrylic paint or ink with matte gel medium. Brush the mixture thickly onto a found object, such as bubble wrap. Print the object onto a surface. Allow it to dry.

Pull the object carefully away from the surface to retain as much texture as possible.

# CREATING BACKGROUND WASHES

Brilliant blue wash with a lot of water

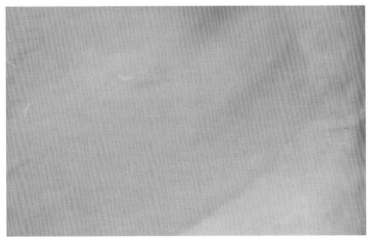

Brilliant blue wash with less water

Create beautiful, soft backgrounds with paint or ink and water. Use just one color per fabric, or blend two or more colors together.

1. Add about a cup of water to a small plastic container. Add a small amount (approximately 1 teaspoon) of soft-body acrylic paint or acrylic ink to the container, and stir thoroughly.

> ### 🔖 NOTE
> *The more water used in the diluted mixture, the paler the final color will be. If you'd like more intense, saturated colors, use less water and more paint or ink. When fabrics dry, they will be lighter than they appear wet. Experiment for the best final result.*

2. Apply diluted color to fabric with a foam brush.

3. Experiment with applying paint to a background that has been moistened with a spray mister, as opposed to painting on dry fabric.

4. For a blended gradation of color, prepare 2 or more colors in separate containers, and apply each color to a fabric in a planned or random pattern.

### ❋ TIP
Splatter or drip a second color on top of the background color for an interesting look.

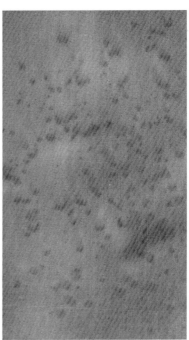

Beetle created with acrylic ink; background stamped with soft-body metallic acrylic paint (pages 24–25), and accented with free-motion stitching

Acrylic inks are thinner and more liquid than acrylic paint, and are fast drying and permanent. They are very highly pigmented and do not change the hand of the fabric very much.

If you mix ink with fabric medium to thicken it, the fabric medium will not change the color, just the viscosity.

## CREATING RANDOM PATTERNS

Tape a piece of plastic wrap to your work surface. Apply a thin layer of ink to the plastic, allowing it to bead up on the surface. Press fabric onto the plastic to pick up the random pattern of dots.

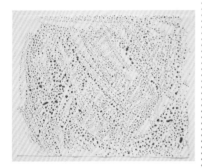

## USING INK AS WATERCOLORS

Create a drawing with a permanent marker and add a watercolor effect over it with diluted acrylic ink.

## TIE "DYEING"

Tie knots around a piece of fabric and dip it into diluted ink for a tie-dye effect.

Tie fabric tightly in various places with string.

Dip the fabric into ink that has been diluted with water.

Cut ties and iron the fabric when dry.

Fabric hand-lettered with acrylic ink and dip pen; image transfer using acrylic paint (page 48)

Ink can be applied to fabric with dip pens for calligraphy, lettering effects, and for pen and ink drawings or with reusable applicator tools to add details or broad strokes of color.

## DIP PEN

**1.** Press fabric to a piece of freezer paper to add stability. Plan out the placement, size, and font of the lettering on a blank piece of paper to use as a guide. Place the lettering guide under the prepared fabric.

**2.** Dip the pen into the ink and brush the bottom edge off against the side of the bottle. Begin lettering, following the guide. Practice on scrap fabric first to get a feeling for the pen. Use even pressure and smooth strokes to complete the lettering, dipping the pen in the ink as needed.

### NOTE

*Do not use acrylic ink in fountain pens. Clean the dip pen before the ink dries to prevent clogging.*

## APPLICATOR TOOLS

**1.** Dip a round- or pointed-tip tool into ink and use like a marker.

**2.** Spray fabric with water and then use an applicator tool to create soft, diffuse lines on dampened fabric.

### NOTE

*The applicator tool does not need to be washed between uses—simply cap it and save it for the next time. Once a tool is used for one color, it should be used for that color every time.*

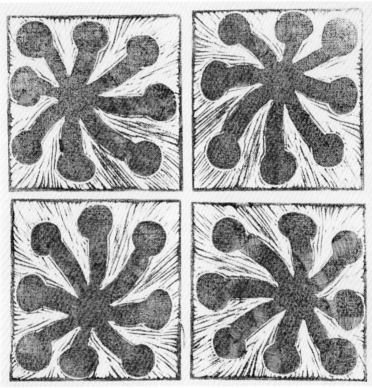

Stamped design using soft-body acrylic paint repeated to create a
secondary pattern

There are a few different ways of using soft-body acrylic paint with handmade or commercial stamps.

1. Apply paint using one of the following techniques:

- Using a paintbrush or foam brush, spread the paint in a thin layer on a shallow plate.

- Gently press the stamp into the paint. Use an up-and-down motion, not a twisting motion, to avoid getting paint in areas where you don't want it.

❋ TIP

It can be helpful to have a slightly padded surface under your fabric to get a crisper stamped image. A layer of thin batting or an old mouse pad works well.

- Apply paint to the stamp with a foam brush, taking care not to overload or flood the stamp with too much paint.

- Roll the paint onto the stamp with a brayer.

2. Firmly press the stamp onto the fabric.

# TECHNIQUE
# PRINTING

Natural grasses printed with soft-body acrylic paint

Natural and found objects can be printed on fabric using soft-body acrylic paint or acrylic ink that has been thickened with fabric medium.

1. Apply a thin layer of paint or thickened ink to a natural or found object with a foam brush. Apply paint smoothly and in several directions to prevent brush strokes from showing.

2. Press the object onto the fabric. It helps to have a slightly padded surface under the fabric to get a crisp print.

- Try applying 2 or more colors to an object, and then print with it.

- Use a printed object to create a background design.

- Use a printed object as a subject.

- Use a printed object to add visual texture.

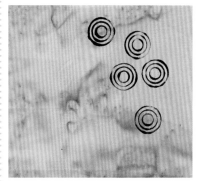

Made with a subtractive monoprinted center and sunprinted (pages 32–33) borders

Monoprinting is the process of making a one-of-a-kind print. In the subtractive method paint is applied to a plate (a smooth surface such as glass, acrylic plate, or vinyl) and then paint is removed to create patterns and designs.

1. Apply a thin layer of paint to the surface of a plate using a foam brush or foam roller. Cover the entire plate.

2. Use combs, stamps, bubble wrap, plastic mesh, bamboo skewers, sponges, and so on to remove paint, creating a pattern or design in the paint on the surface.

 TIP

Acrylic paint dries quickly, so work fast or add a little matte gel medium to the paint to increase the amount of time with which you have to work.

3. Carefully place fabric on top of the plate.

 TIP

Flexible vinyl such as Quilter's Vinyl is easy to use for monoprinting.

4. Cover the fabric with a piece of parchment paper, freezer paper, or palette paper. Using an old rolling pin or a hard brayer, apply even pressure all over the surface of the plate to transfer the paint from the plate to the fabric.

5. Slowly peel off the fabric from the plate, and set it aside to dry. The plate can be painted again (if you are using the same or similar colors), or washed and new colors applied.

Made with an additive monoprint center, painted over with a diluted
wash of color

In the additive monoprint method, paint is applied to a plate (a smooth surface such as glass, acrylic plate, or vinyl).

1. If you want to plan out your design, trace the outline of the plate on a piece of paper and draw a design within the outline.

2. Place the paper under the plate and use it as a guide to apply paint, or apply paint free-hand to the plate.

3. When you are satisfied with the placement of paint on the plate, carefully place fabric on top of the plate.

4. Cover the fabric with a piece of parchment paper, freezer paper, or palette paper. Using an old rolling pin or a hard brayer, apply even pressure all over the surface of the plate to transfer the paint from the plate to the fabric.

5. Slowly peel off the fabric from the plate and set it aside to dry. The plate can be painted again (if you are using the same or similar colors), or washed and new colors applied.

### ❋ TIP

Additive and subtractive monoprinting can be combined on the same plate or fabric. For example, create a subtractive design on a plate and then add a painted design to it before printing onto fabric. Or print a subtractive design onto fabric and then print an additive design onto the same fabric.

# SUNPRINTING

Made with sunprinted fabric using leaves, salt, and blended colors

Transparent and translucent soft-body acrylic paints are great for sunprints (check the bottle to see what type of paint you have).

1. Mix transparent or translucent acrylic paint to a consistency of 3 parts water, 1 part paint.

## ❋ TIP

Learn to experiment with different consistencies of paint and water for different effects.

2. Place white fabric on thin plastic to protect the work area. Spray the fabric lightly with water to dampen it. Apply paint to the dampened fabric.

3. Either place objects on the fabric to create distinct sharp patterns or scrunch fabric up to create areas of light and dark as the fabric dries. When placing objects on the fabric, make sure the object edges are firmly in touch with the fabric or you will get blurry edges.

4. If desired, toss sea or rock salt onto the surface of the wet fabric to create starburst effects.

5. Place the fabric in direct sunlight. Bright, clear, warm days will yield the best sunprints.

6. Remove the items, brush off the salt, and iron out the creases.

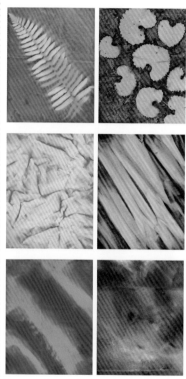

Top row from left: fabric with leaves, fabric with leaves and sea salt effects

Middle row from left: fabric scrunched up while wet, fabric finger-pleated when wet

Bottom row from left: two colors applied in a pattern, four different colors blended

# TECHNIQUE
# STENCILING

Stenciled image made with soft-body acrylic paint, accented with quilting

An image created with stencils has crisp, sharp, clean edges.

1. Draw a design on paper with closed areas, that is, all the shapes are separate and enclosed. Determine how many colors the finished design will have.

2. Cut out freezer-paper pieces about the same size as your drawing paper. Cut the same number of freezer-paper sheets as the number of colors in the design. For example, if the design has 4 colors, you'll need 4 sheets of freezer paper.

3. Stack the freezer-paper sheets, shiny side down, under the drawing paper, carefully lining up the top edges. Using a hole punch, punch a hole in 2 of the upper corners through all the layers. These holes are used to register, or line up, the colors when applying the paint.

4. Place 1 piece of freezer paper over the drawing (shiny side down), line up the registration holes, and trace all the shapes in the first color. Label this piece of freezer paper #1. Set it aside.

5. Place another piece of freezer paper over the drawing (shiny side down), line up the registration holes, and trace all the shapes in the second color. Label this piece of freezer paper #2. Set it aside. Repeat for all the remaining sheets of freezer paper and colors on your drawing. The more precise you are when tracing and cutting, the more exact the registration of the final image will be.

**6.** Neatly and carefully cut out all the shapes on all the pieces of freezer paper with a craft knife such as an X-ACTO knife.

**7.** Iron freezer paper #1 to the fabric. Very lightly mark with a pencil through the registration holes in the freezer paper onto the fabric.

**8.** Using a stencil brush, apply soft-body acrylic paint to the openings in the freezer paper. Carefully remove the freezer paper, and allow the paint to dry to the touch.

**9.** Iron freezer paper #2 to the fabric, lining up the marks on the fabric with the registration holes in the freezer paper.

**10.** Again apply paint to the open areas, remove the freezer paper, and allow the paint to dry. Repeat with all the pieces of freezer paper and colors to complete the design.

**✳ TIP**

If you carefully remove the used freezer paper to avoid tearing it, you can use it again after it's dry.

# MORE IDEAS FOR STENCILING

- Use metallic acrylic paint for some or all areas of your design.

Two shades of metallic silver paint and two shades of blue acrylic paint were used to create this tricycle.

- Combine the stenciling technique with other techniques and materials for unique effects

1. Paint a color through a cut stencil and allow it to dry.

2. Before removing the stencil, splatter a second color over the first color. Remove the stencil after the second color is dry.

3. Use a commercial or handmade stamp to add details or a pattern to the splattered color.

4. Complete the image with the remaining stencils.

- Alter a commercial fabric with stenciled images to create depth and visual interest.

Two different were colors were stenciled on commercial batik fabric.

Fusible web background painted with soft-body acrylic paint; flower painted with acrylic ink (pages 20–21)

Soft-body acrylic paint and acrylic ink are not just for fabric! Experiment with other surfaces for unique effects. Timtex and fast2fuse are two heavyweight interfacings that are marvelous when painted. Lutradur is a thin, translucent interfacing that is ideal for painting, stamping, and transfers.

## PAINTING ON TIMTEX AND FAST2FUSE

1. Cut a piece of Timtex as a background.

2. Seal the Timtex with a thin coat of matte gel medium, and allow it to dry.

### 🗒 NOTE

*Coating (or priming) a porous surface such as Timtex allows the paint applied in the next step to remain vibrant and any lines or shapes to stay sharp and clear. You will also need less paint, as it will not be absorbed into the surface of the Timtex.*

3. Apply paint or ink all over the Timtex, as desired.

4. Cut another piece of Timtex.

5. Apply paint or ink directly to the uncoated Timtex, and compare it to the coated Timtex. Repeat with a piece of fast2fuse. Because fast2fuse has fusible attached to both sides, it is not necessary to coat it.

**Soft-body acrylic paint on (from Top): fast2fuse, coated Timtex, uncoated Timtex**

## PAINTING ON LUTRADUR

1. Paint a piece of Lutradur with paint or ink, diluted as a wash or full strength. Allow it to dry.

**Painted Lutradur with image transfer**

 TIP

Because the Lutradur is such an open fiber, place a piece of fabric under it when painting. Excess paint will pass through the Lutradur, creating an interesting design on the fabric below.

2. Use this piece of painted Lutradur as a base for other techniques, such as stamping (pages 24–25), image transferring (pages 46–48), printing (pages 26–27), and so forth. Cut or tear the Lutradur into shapes to use in your work.

## PAINTING ON FUSIBLE WEB

Applying shapes made from painted fusible web adds an unusual, organic touch to your work.

1. Apply diluted paint or ink to a piece of fusible web, and allow it to dry.

**Painted and stamped Lutradur**

2. Cut or tear the painted fusible into the desired shapes.

3. Place the painted fusible on the fabric, covering it with parchment paper or a pressing sheet. If you are using paper-backed fusible, place it paint side down. Fuse in place with a dry iron.

4. If you are using paper-backed fusible, allow it to cool completely before removing the paper.

**Lutradur background painted and stamped with soft-body acrylic paint, using a gel medium appliqué shape (pages 15–16), and a gel medium image transfer (pages 46–48)**

# USING WATER-SOLUBLE INK PENCILS

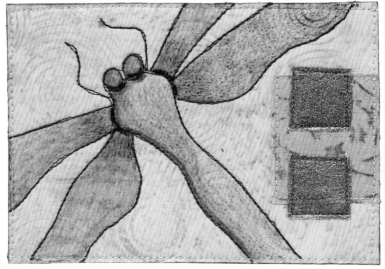

Quilted dragonfly colored with Derwent Inktense pencils and Angelina fiber squares painted with metallic acrylic ink

Use water-soluble ink pencils and watercolor pencils to create translucent washes, watercolor effects, and brilliant or subtle images.

1. Draw on fabric using the pencils.

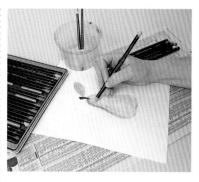

2. With a paintbrush dipped in water, blend and shade the colors together. The water will intensify the colors. More water will result in lighter colors and more spreading; less water will result in deeper colors and less spreading or bleeding.

### ❋ TIP

If the pencils run or bleed too much, remember that stitching can help define the finished images.

3. Add more pencil lines to the wet drawing for more intense colors, or allow the drawing to dry thoroughly before adding more color.

Commercial fabric painted with soft-body acrylic paint and acrylic ink

Once you own a piece of fabric, you can do anything you want to it!

- Tone down a bright fabric with a diluted wash of color using soft-body acrylic paint or acrylic ink.

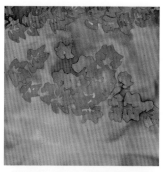

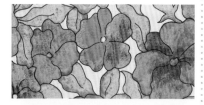

A warm yellow wash tones down the fabric.

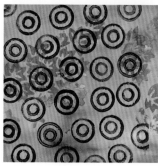

Batik stamped with acrylic paint

- Emphasize an area of a print using paint, ink, or colored pencils.

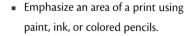

Painted-in motifs change the character of the fabric.

 TIP

Black-and-white prints in particular lend themselves to modification.

Print painted with diluted acrylic paint

# TECHNIQUE
# MAKING IMAGE TRANSFERS

Inkjet-printed image transferred with gel medium

There are many ways to add images and text to your work; image transfers are fast and easy. Transferred images tend to be lighter than the original image, so adjust the saturation level in your photo editing program to be deeper and more intense, and use the "photo" or "best" setting on your printer.

## GEL MEDIUM TRANSFER

1. Print an image (color or black-and-white) onto an overhead transparency with an inkjet printer.

 NOTE

*There are different types of overhead transparencies; you need to use one that is meant for inkjet printers.*

2. Cut out the image, leaving space around it.

3. Apply a thin, even layer of matte gel medium or fabric medium to the fabric, covering about the same area as the printed image.

4. Place the printed image facedown on the fresh matte medium. Rub the back of the image with a burnisher or a spoon.

5. Lift a corner of the transparency to see whether the ink is transferring to the medium. If it is, remove the transparency. If it isn't, burnish the back of the image a little longer. If the image hasn't transferred at all, you may have used too little medium or waited too long and it dried. If the image smears, you used too much medium. Experiment for best results.

**6.** When the medium dries, the image is permanently captured on the fabric.

### ❋ TIPS

■ The transferring process reverses the printed image, so remember to reverse the image when printing on the transparency if it will matter, such as when you are using text.

■ Don't iron directly over a transfer. Cover it first with a pressing sheet or piece of parchment paper.

## ACRYLIC PAINT IMAGE TRANSFERS

**1.** Print the desired image, in reverse, on paper using a **laser** printer. Cut out the paper close to the image.

**2.** Using white acrylic paint, cover an area on the fabric that is the same size as the image.

**3.** Place the image face-down on top of the fresh paint, and press it down to ensure good contact. Allow the paper and paint to dry completely.

**4.** Spray the back of the paper with water. Allow the water to sit on the paper in a puddle for a minute.

**5.** Gently rub off the softened paper using your finger. Rub until all of the paper is removed.

PROJECTS

You will soon discover how truly fortunate you really are.
Lucky Numbers  44, 24, 35, 16, 8, 27

*Sprig,* made by Jane Dávila

TECHNIQUES: Painted Lutradur background, stamped motif, paint-washed found paper, matte gel medium used as adhesive

### Supplies

- Piece of Lutradur larger than 2½″ × 3½″
- Scraps of fabric and paper
- Soft-body acrylic paints
- Matte gel medium
- Foam paintbrushes
- Small found object (such as a watch gear, as used in this project)
- Handmade or purchased stamp

1. Paint the Lutradur with one or more colors of the paint (page 40). Allow it to dry thoroughly, and cut it to 2½″ × 3½″.

2. Using a foam brush, apply the paint to a stamp, and print onto fabric (pages 24–25).

3. When the paint is dry, carefully cut out the stamped motif about ⅛″ from the edge.

4. Apply a diluted wash of paint over an interesting piece of paper (pages 18–19). I used a fortune-cookie fortune.

5. Use matte gel medium to adhere all parts to the Lutradur (pages 15–16).

## ✿ TIPS

- If you are making many cards to trade, paint one large piece of Lutradur, and then cut it into 2½″ × 3½″ pieces.

- If you are using a large stamp, you may only need to paint a section of it prior to printing.

- When applying gel medium to a very small item (such as a watch gear), place the item on a protected surface—freezer paper or parchment paper works well—brush on the medium, and use tweezers to pick up and place the item on your ATC (artist trading card).

*Fleur,* made by Jane Dávila

TECHNIQUES: Water-soluble ink pencils accented with
free-motion quilting

### Supplies

- fast2fuse 4" × 6" rectangle
- Scraps of fabric, some at least 4" × 6"
- Water-soluble ink pencils such as Derwent Inktense pencils
- Small paintbrush
- Variety of colors of thread

# FABRIC POSTCARD

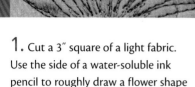

**1.** Cut a 3" square of a light fabric. Use the side of a water-soluble ink pencil to roughly draw a flower shape in the center of the fabric square.

**2.** Dip a small paintbrush in water, and, starting from the center of the flower, spread the color around. Add more water to the center, and allow it to wick and spread the color toward the outer edges of the fabric square.

**3.** Use another water-soluble ink pencil to add a small amount of color to the center of the flower shape. Set the fabric aside to dry.

**4.** Fuse a background onto the 4" × 6" piece of fast2fuse. Add other pieces of fabric in various sizes and shapes as desired. Sew in place.

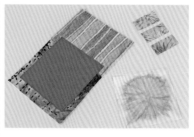

**5.** After the flower is dry, iron it to flatten and heat set it. Sew it onto the postcard background. Use free-motion quilting to define the petals and center of the flower.

**6.** Iron fabric to the back of the postcard, adding an address and message if you wish. To finish, sew through all the layers around the perimeter of the outside edge.

*Common Pear,* made by Jane Dávila

TECHNIQUES: **Stenciling, image transfers**

### Supplies

- Fabric for background, border, binding, and backing
- Thin, sturdy batting
- Freezer paper
- Hole punch
- Soft-body acrylic paints
- Stencil brushes
- Matte gel medium
- Text printed on transparency sheet (pages 46–48)

**1.** Create a stenciled image of a pear by following the instructions on pages 34–36.

**2.** After the paint is dry, add text using the gel medium transfer technique (pages 46–48).

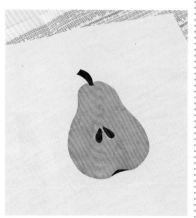

**3.** Trim the background fabric, and add borders.

**4.** Layer, baste, quilt, and finish the edges.

## ❋ TIP

Keep in mind that if the stenciled image is not perfectly lined up, or registered, quilting lines can hide any imperfections.

*La Luciernaga,* made by Jane Dávila

TECHNIQUES: **Stamped image, painted sandpaper accents**

### Supplies

- Fabric for background
- Fabric (cotton and silk) and paper for collaged elements
- Thin, sturdy batting
- Soft-body acrylic paints

- Handmade or purchased stamp
- Foam paintbrushes
- Sandpaper (120-grit works well)
- Seed beads
- Gallery-wrapped prestretched canvas

1. Using a foam brush, apply the paint to a stamp, and print on the fabric (pages 24–25).

2. Using another foam brush, apply the paint to the sandpaper.

3. Cut the sandpaper into small squares using a rotary cutter. Painted sandpaper has the visual appearance of Ultrasuede, and because you paint it, it can be any color you like.

###  NOTE

*Save old rotary cutter blades that no longer work on fabric for cutting rougher materials such as sandpaper.*

4. Cut the background and batting. Add other pieces of fabric and paper, plus stamped images, as desired. Use a gluestick to hold the sandpaper squares in place for sewing. After the sewing is complete, add seed beads.

###  NOTE

*A typical home sewing machine will easily sew through sandpaper—after all, it's designed to sew through multiple layers of heavy material such as denim. However, I do recommend that you change the needle when you've finished!*

5. Paint a gallery-wrapped pre-stretched canvas with acrylic paint, and allow it to dry thoroughly. Attach the completed quilt to the canvas by sewing through the quilt and into the canvas at several points.

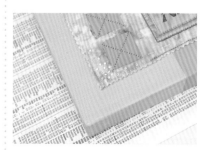

*Wildflowers,* made by Jane Dávila

TECHNIQUES: **Diluted acrylic ink, free-motion quilting**

**Supplies**

- Pencil
- White fabric for background
- Thin, sturdy batting
- Acrylic inks
- Paintbrush
- Felt
- Black thread and thread to match or contrast with finished background

**1.** Draw a sketch on paper. Trace the sketch onto the white fabric.

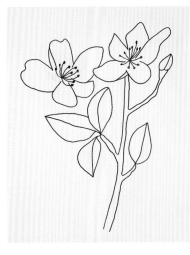

**2.** Layer the fabric with batting (no backing is needed at this point), and free-motion quilt on the sketched lines with black thread.

**3.** Apply diluted ink to the various parts of the stitched sketch (page 21). Then apply a background color, working from the outside edges toward the sketch.

### ❋ TIP

Apply much less color than you think you need; the diluted ink will spread and grow outside the stitched lines. Wait a few minutes to determine whether you need to add more ink. The blending and mingling of colors adds to the whole effect, so just let go—whatever happens, happens.

**4.** Trim the painting when it is completely dry. Layer it on top of a piece of felt, and sew the layers together using a buttonhole or blanket stitch and a matching or contrasting thread. Once the layers are attached, trim the felt to a pleasing dimension to act visually as a border, although it is also the backing.

*Trinket,* made by Jane Dávila

**TECHNIQUES: Painting, stamping, printing**

### Supplies

- Fabric
- Soft-body acrylic paints
- Handmade or purchased stamp
- Found object for printing
- Foam paintbrushes
- Bag pattern (refer to the pattern for fabric quantities and other supplies)

# PROJECT
# PAINTED FASHION ACCESSORY

**1.** Determine how much yardage needs to be painted based on the pattern.

**2.** Paint the background with the paint. Allow it to dry.

**3.** Using a foam brush, apply paint to a stamp, and print it all over the painted background fabric (pages 24–25). Allow it to dry.

**4.** Using a foam brush, apply paint to the found object, and print it all over the painted, stamped fabric (pages 26–27).

### ◤ NOTE
*Create a fabric with a lot of visual depth by adding layers of texture and color.*

**5.** Cut out the pieces you need to make the bag from the completed fabric. Construct the bag, following the pattern instructions.

### ✳ TIP
Painted fabric has the stiffness and hand of home décor–weight fabric and is ideal for patterns calling for that weight. Be aware that painted fabric abrades, so you would not want to use it on anything that gets a lot of heavy use.

*Natura,* made by Jane Dávila

TECHNIQUES: **Painting, printing, matte gel medium adhesive, image transfer**

### Supplies

- Canvas book
- Soft-body acrylic paints
- Handmade or purchased stamps
- Fabric, papers, and found objects

- Matte gel medium
- Foam paintbrushes
- Images printed on transparency sheets (pages 46–48)
- Small piece of heavy-duty fusible web

# CANVAS BOOK

**1.** Paint the cover of the canvas book with full-strength paint.

 NOTE

*Different fabrics absorb paint at different rates. For example, unprimed canvas absorbs more paint than quilting-weight cotton.*

**2.** Apply washes of paint to the inside pages of the book (pages 18–19). If the washes appear too dark, blot off some color with a crumpled paper towel.

**3.** Add collage elements to the front cover by cutting shapes from cotton fabric and applying them to the canvas with matte gel medium. Add more elements to the inside pages.

Left page: stamped design and image transfer; right page: screen print on batik fabric and found paper with wash of diluted paint

Left page: stamped design and found objects; right page: printed miniature pears

**4.** Back a strip of fabric with heavy-duty fusible web. Cut it 2″ wide by the height of the book. Fuse it over the spine of the book and on the front and back cover to finish.

# GALLERY

## Judy Coates Perez

*Avian Love Shack,*
made by Judy Coates Perez,
6″ × 10½″

**Mixed-media piece made with Timtex, acrylic paints, and hand-embossed aluminum craft metal**

*Blogs:* judyperez.blogspot.com
paintthreadsprojects.blogspot.com
*Email:* judycoatesperez@gmail.com

*Jewels of the Garden,* made by Judy Coates Perez, 8″ × 6″
**Wholecloth painted quilt made with acrylic inks and aloe vera gel**

# Virginia A. Spiegel

Art cloth made
by Virginia A. Spiegel

**Art cloth made with acrylic
paint, screen printed and
stamped in layers**

Art cloth made by
Virginia A. Spiegel

**Art cloth made with acrylic
paint, screen printed and
stamped in layers**

*Website:* virginiaspiegel.com

## ▣ Terry Grant

*Hazle on Graduation Day*, made by Terry Grant, 13¼" × 17"

**Appliqué quilt made with pastel pencils**

*Crow*, made by Terry Grant, 11¼" × 11¼"

**Fused appliqué quilt made with hand-stamped fabrics**

*Blog:* andsewitgoes.blogspot.com

# ◉ Jane LaFazio

*Bird on a Pear*, made by Jane LaFazio, 4" × 4"

**Mixed-media piece on canvas, made with acrylic paint, colored pencils, and gel medium transfers**

*Molinillo Quiltlet*, made by Jane LaFazio, 4" × 4"

**Canvas quilt made with acrylic paint and hand-carved stamps**

*Website:* www.PlainJaneStudio.com
*Blog:* janeville.blogspot.com

*Piterskoie Okno/St Pete Window 22*, made by Natalya Aikens, 10¼" × 5" × 1½"

**Mixed-media diptych on canvas, made with acrylic paint, colored pencils, and gel medium image transfers**

*Piterskoie Okno/St Pete Window 18*, made by Natalya Aikens, 11" × 11"

**Quilt made with vintage textile, acrylic paint, watercolor pencils, and gel medium image transfer**

*Website:* www.artbynatalya.com

*Blog:* artbynatalya.blogspot.com

# ● Jane Dávila

*Apidae,*
made by Jane Dávila,
6¾″ × 10″

**Quilt made with acrylic paint,
screen printed and stamped
images, and found objects**

*Haste,* made by Jane Dávila, 10¼″ × 10¼″
**Quilt made with acrylic paint, stamped images, and found paper**

## ● Elin Waterston

*Pisces 2*, made by Elin Waterston, 8½″ × 8½″

**Quilt made with acrylic paint and screen-printed images**

*Isia Isabella*,
made by Elin Waterston,
7½″ × 11½″

**Quilt made with acrylic paint
and block-printed images**

*Website:* www.elinwaterston.com
*Blog:* willlovelogic.blogspot.com

# ■ Lynn Koolish

*Water Lilies #4,* made by Lynn Koolish, 12½″ × 9½″

Quilt made with acrylic paint, gel medium image transfer, painted Lutradur, and cotton

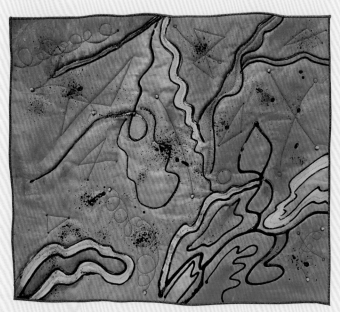

*Water, No Lilies,* made by Lynn Koolish, 17″ × 15″

Quilt made with acrylic paint with beaded embellishment

*Website:* www.lynnkoolish.com

*Email:* lynn@lynnkoolish.com

# ABOUT THE AUTHOR

Jane Dávila began her professional art career as a printmaker, specializing in etchings and intaglios. She was a studio artist for many years, exhibiting at commercial galleries and having her work placed in many private and corporate collections worldwide. She switched to fiber and quilting in the 1990s but still incorporates many printmaking techniques in her work. Jane teaches art quilting and surface design workshops nationally. Jane lives in Ridgefield, Connecticut, with her husband, Carlos, an oil painter and sculptor.

Visit Jane at her website, www.janedavila.com, or her blog, janedavila.blogspot.com.

*Also by Jane Dávila*

For art quilting supplies:

FLOURISH!–COUNTRY QUILTER
P.O. Box 344
Georgetown, CT 06877
(203) 438-0926
(888) 277-7780
info@countryquilter.com
www.countryquilter.com

For a list of other fine books from C&T Publishing, visit our website to view our catalog online:

## C&T PUBLISHING, INC.

P.O. Box 1456
Lafayette, CA 94549
(800) 284-1114

Email: ctinfo@ctpub.com
Website: www.ctpub.com

C&T Publishing's professional photography services are now available to the public. Visit us at www.ctmediaservices.com.

**Tips and Techniques** can be found at www.ctpub.com > Consumer Resources > Quiltmaking Basics: Tips & Techniques for Quiltmaking & More
For quilting supplies:

## COTTON PATCH

1025 Brown Ave.
Lafayette, CA 94549
Store: (925) 284-1177
Mail order: (925) 283-7883

Email: CottonPa@aol.com
Website: www.quiltusa.com